How Do Hang Gliders Work?

Jennifer Boothroyd

Lerner Publications Company
Minneapolis

For Maddie
and McKenna

Lerner Publications Company
A division of Lerner Publishing Group, Inc.
241 First Avenue North
Minneapolis, MN 55401 U.S.A.

Website address: www.lernerbooks.com

Library of Congress Cataloging-in-Publication Data

Boothroyd, Jennifer, 1972–
    How do hang gliders work? / by Jennifer Boothroyd.
        pages   cm. — (Lightning Bolt Books™—How Flight Works)
    Includes index.
    ISBN 978-0-7613-8970-5 (lib. bdg. : alk. paper)
        1. Hang gliding—Juvenile literature. 2. Hang gliders—Juvenile literature. 3. Gliders
(Aeronautics)—Piloting—Juvenile literature. I. Title.
    TL765.B66 2013
    629.1'4—dc23   2012020001

Manufactured in the United States of America
1 — MG — 12/31/12

Table of Contents

What Is a Hang Glider?

A kite soars high
into the air.
It dives.
It swoops.

Imagine you could ride a kite. Feel the wind. See the treetops. Sound like fun? Then take a ride on a hang glider.

This hang glider is high in the sky!

A hang glider is an
unpowered aircraft.
That means it
flies without
a motor.

The largest part of a hang glider is the wing. The wing is a metal frame covered with fabric. The fabric creates a sail.

The sail can be many different colors.

A harness hangs below the wing.
The pilot rides in the harness.
The pilot uses the control
bar to steer the glider.

This is the
control bar.

Safety gear is important!

Hang glider pilots use a lot of safety gear. Pilots wear helmets, goggles, and flight suits.

A small computer on the hang glider tells a pilot the glider's speed, height, and direction.

The computer tells the pilot where he is.

Harnesses have parachutes.
A parachute helps a
pilot land safely in
an emergency.

Getting off the Ground

Ready for takeoff? The pilot straps into the harness. He grabs the control bar. He runs off the edge of a hill or ramp.

The sail of the glider catches the air. Takeoff! The glider soars.

The pilot puts her legs in the harness once she is in the air.

But gravity is pulling on the glider. Gravity is a force that pulls objects toward the ground.

Apples fall to the ground because gravity is pulling on them.

The combination of gravity and lift makes the glider move through the air.

lift

gravity

A glider needs lift to stay in the air. Lift is a force that works against gravity. Air flowing over the wing creates lift.

Glider pilots also find other types of lift. Gliders rise in spots of very warm air. **This is called thermal lift.**

thermal lift

Pilots must learn ways to find thermal lift.

Ridge lift happens when air hits a hillside and is pushed up.

Pilots like to launch off a hillside. They can use the ridge lift to help get airborne.

Keep Soaring

How does the pilot control the hang glider?

The pilot's harness hangs from the keel.

This is the keel. The pilot hangs below in the harness.

The pilot holds the control bar. He uses the bar to push and pull his body in all directions.

Steering in a harness is similar to controlling a tire swing.

You can move in any direction, not just forward and backward.

This is called weight shifting.

The pilot moves his body right or left to tip the wing sideways. The hang glider turns toward the lower side.

This is called a roll.

Tipping the front of the glider up or down controls the speed. This up or down direction is called pitch. The pilot pulls her body forward to lower the front of the glider. This makes the glider move faster.

The pilot pushes her body backward to raise the front of the glider. This makes the glider move slower.

A Smooth Landing

A pilot finds a good spot to land. She gets closer to the ground. She takes her feet out of the harness.

Hang gliders need 50 to 200 feet (15 to 61 meters) of flat, clear ground to land safely.

The pilot pushes the control
bar forward. The wing tips
up. It pushes against the air.
The glider stalls.

The pilot's feet touch the ground. The pilot runs with the glider. The glider slowly comes to a stop. Today's ride is done. **Wasn't it fun?**

Landing a glider is tricky. It takes lots of practice to land smoothly.

Parts of a Hang Glider

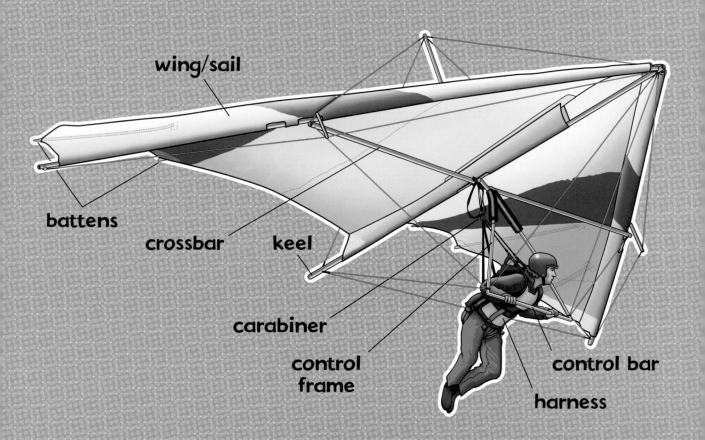

wing/sail

battens

crossbar

keel

carabiner

control frame

control bar

harness

Fun Facts

- Hang gliders can launch from flat ground. They are pulled by a truck or a small plane. They are let go when they are high in the air.

- Hang gliders have traveled more than 400 miles (644 kilometers) in a single flight.

- Racing hang gliders reach speeds of 55 miles (90 km) per hour.

- Modern hang gliders became popular in the 1960s.

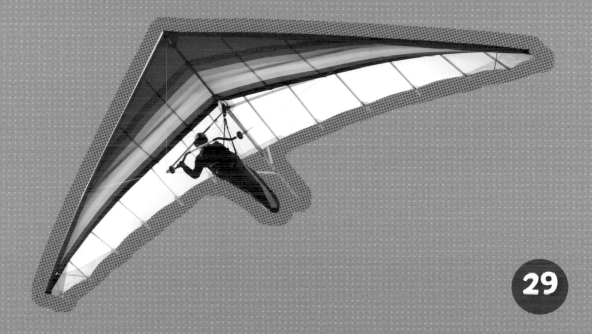

Glossary

aircraft: a vehicle that travels in the air

gravity: a force that pulls an object toward the ground

keel: the center support pole of a hang glider

lift: a force that pushes objects up in the air

parachute: a device made of fabric that slows an object or a person when falling from a height

roll: tipping the glider sideways to turn it right or left

sail: the large piece of fabric covering a hang glider's frame

thermal: an area of warm, rising air

Further Reading

FAI: Hang and Paragliding
World Records
http://www.fai.org/record-hang-gliding-and
-paragliding

Hicks, Kelli L. *Hang Gliding and Paragliding.* Vero Beach, FL: Rouke, 2010.

NASA Glenn Research Center: The Beginner's Guide to Aeronautics
http://www.grc.nasa.gov/WWW/K-12/airplane

Silverman, Buffy. *How Do Hot Air Balloons Work?* Minneapolis: Lerner Publications Company, 2013.

Smithsonian National Air and Space Museum: How Things Fly
http://howthingsfly.si.edu/activities/forces-flight

Whittall, Noel. *Hang Gliding.* New York: Gareth Stevens, 2008.

Index

Photo Acknowledgments

The images in this book are used with the permission of: © Neale Cousland/Dreamstime.com, p. 1; © iStockphoto.com/P_Wei, p. 2; © Emmerich-Webb/Photonica/Getty Images, p. 4; © Joe McBride/Stone/Getty Images, p. 5; © iStockphoto.com/Daniel Cardiff, pp. 6, 29; © Dennis Hallinan/Alamy, p. 7; © Bill Losh/Taxi/Getty Images, p. 8; © Dennis MacDonald/Alamy, p. 9; © Glow Images, p. 10; © Oliver Furrer/Photographers Choice RF/Getty Images, p. 11; © Aleksandra Lande/Dreamstime.com, p. 12; © Galen Rowell/CORBIS, p. 13; © iStockphoto.com/GoodMood Photo, p. 14; © Michael Kemp/RubberBall/Glow Images, p. 15; © Caterina Bernardi/CORBIS, p. 16; © Leo Mason/CORBIS, p. 17; Elan Sunstar/DanitaDelmont.com/Newscom, p. 18; © Lisa Mckelvie/Photolibrary/Getty Images, p. 19; © Cheryl Casey/Dreamstime.com, p. 20; © David Fleetham/Taxi/Getty Images, p. 21; © imac/Alamy, p. 22; © Cusp/SuperStock, pp. 23, 24; © Jules Frazier Photography/UpperCut Images/Getty Images, p. 25; Josh Noel/Chicago Tribune/MCT/Newscom, p. 26; © 2011 aluha/Bigstock.com, p. 27; © Laura Westlund/Independent Picture Service, p. 28; © Caterina Bernardi/Taxi/Getty Images, p. 30; © Gary Conner/Photolibrary/Getty Images, p. 31.

Front cover: © iStockphoto.com/Steven Robertson.

Main body text set in Johann Light 30/36.